Introduction..2

Acknowledgements...4

Section One
Understanding How the Mind Works 5

Section Two
How Our Words Can Influence a Medical Situation..........20

Section Three
Teachers and Sales Professionals..34

Section Four
Parents and Partners...52

Section Five
Things We Silently Say to Ourselves..................................63

Bibliography...76

About the Author..78

Introduction

Say This, Not That offers an easy-to-understand explanation of how our minds work. It is designed to help you understand how powerful words can be so that you can choose your words more wisely. You'll notice when you put more thought into what you say, you will become more influential and a better communicator with family, friends, customers, business associates, and even yourself.

This book is sprinkled with short, simple examples of what to say and what not to say. It is designed to open your mind to possibilities. You will learn to easily incorporate language patterns into your everyday life. These patterns will help you to become more persuasive in natural and subtle ways.

You will discover that using these new patterns will make your life and the lives of those around you easier and more pleasant, because you will be able to speak with tact, direction and a higher level of Emotional Intelligence (EQ is the ability to perceive and handle the emotions of one's self and the emotions of others.)

Although Intelligence Quotient (IQ) is important, research has shown that, in business, as well as in your personal life, having EQ is even more important. (Goleman 1996)

> Mindy, I want to thank you for your hypnotherapy sessions and expertise in helping me to overcome my "limiting beliefs". I have been noticing significant changes in my business and client attraction. None of my previous efforts have had much success until I started working with you, so I am grateful that I discovered hypnotherapy via your expertise. Take care and thank you.
>
>   S.E.C. Honolulu, Hawaii

Acknowledgements

I am very grateful to my loving and supportive parents Robert Ash and Barbara Ash. My mom was very instrumental in encouraging me to complete this book.

I give special thanks to my consultant Dr. Ginger Marable; my sister, Tracy Ash, who assisted me in editing and proof reading. And thank you to my friend Sonia Higgins for her creative eye. Thank you to George Johnson for his words of encouragement. And to my dear friend Terra Roisin who assisted with conceptual ideas for the cover as well as editing.

Additionally, I am grateful to my friends and colleagues Will Goodey and Robert Jackson for their dedication to helping people create better lives.

I am thankful for the brilliant and caring people that I have quoted in this book because they too are committed to helping people better themselves.

Section One

Understanding How The Mind Works

When I was sixteen years old I had an incredible body, as many teenage girls do. I was slender, fit and toned as a result of spending at least 10 hours a week in a jazz, ballet or tap dance class, along with a regular routine of walking to school, playing racquetball and sailing during the summer. I weighed about 115 pounds, which was fine for my bone structure and body type. At that time, I was dating a man who was 10 years older than I. He was a bit smug and arrogant, and one day commented: "Why are your fingers so long and slender while the rest of you is not? Your butt is getting fat." Within one week my weight shot up to 125 pounds and it continued to creep up over the next several years.

Back then I remember laying in bed in the morning thinking, "What am I going to eat today on my diet?" My focus was entirely on food. By noontime I was already out of control, even eating a whole cake in one day, slice by thin slice by thin slice until the whole thing was gone and I felt disgusting! I would clean out the freezer and throw away freezer-burned piecrust and then later pick it out of the trash and eat it. Obviously, I had a real problem.

For years I struggled, with my weight fluctuating between 130 and 145 pounds. I would drop a few pounds and then gain them back plus more. This yo-yo pattern continued for several years until I was about 21, and then another very attractive man said the right thing to me. The weight started to come off and stay off, and I finally gained control. (You'll learn what was said later in the book, so stay tuned.)

I never understood why I struggled with my weight from age 16 to 21 until I began my career as a Hypnotherapist. Now, when I reflect back to one of the most miserable times in my life I finally realize how the problem started, and what brought the emotional rollercoaster and overeating to an end, as well as what was needed to turn my life around and keep my weight where I want it to be: I used to be a "live-to-eat", person and shifted into an "eat-to- live" person.

Now, don't get me wrong, I still enjoy food and I eat whatever I want, only now I typically eat reasonably sized portions because I am in control mentally and emotionally. I really do enjoy being healthy, slender and attractive and those good feelings are much greater than any pleasure I get from food. Actually, in the past food was more like instant gratification followed by pain, along with disappointment, guilt and shame.

Most people have no idea how their mind works, so they live in a knee-jerk responsive manner, always reacting to what life throws at them, feeling like they are just victims of circumstance. Many of us cycle through cliché thoughts such as, "Life is a struggle," or "I just look at food and get fat," or "No one said it was going to be easy." Usually people let their thoughts and feelings run amok, with their mind running them instead of the other way around. One moment they're feeling depressed and frustrated, and shortly after they're feeling happy. But as it turns out, our ability to rapidly change emotional states is a good thing. Just as quickly as we can become stressed out and frustrated, we can just as easily become calm and relaxed. Our emotions can change rapidly, depending on what we are paying attention to and focusing on.

In this book you will learn more about how your mind works, and with this information you will be able to start taking charge of your thoughts, feelings and behaviors so that you will be able to feel calmer, more in control and happier more often. This new knowledge will also help you to become a better communicator with those around you.

Our minds work on a couple of different levels: We have our conscious mind and we have our *subconscious* or *unconscious* mind (those terms are interchangeable). At a deep level we have our super-conscious mind that is the intuitive, divine wisdom within each one of us. The conscious mind does very little. We think with our conscious mind and we make decisions and plans with our conscious mind. It is where our short-term memory is located, as well as our willpower.

Naturally, we want to think that we are consciously in control of everything, but the truth is we are not. We primarily run on autopilot. When we try to make behavioral changes consciously, we have to think about them first.

For example, many people will break free from a bad habit, such as smoking cigarettes or biting their fingernails, and when they accomplish this with their willpower they are doing it consciously; basically they have to think about avoiding the negative behavioral pattern every time the urge surfaces.

Habits like smoking and nail biting are located in the subconscious mind. You can break free from these habits with willpower; however, this means you have to think about it and so you are actually focusing on what you *don't* want rather than what you *do* want and that is why it can be difficult with willpower. Many people don't realize negative habits can be eliminated much more easily and quickly by communicating with the subconscious mind using hypnosis.

The subconscious mind is not only where our habits are located, but also our emotions, our imagination and our long-term memory. Our subconscious is our survival mind, and it protects us both physically and emotionally. Think about this: if you stepped off the curb and a car was coming you wouldn't consciously think to yourself "what should I do?" You would step back onto the curb automatically. That is your subconscious protecting you physically. It is a brilliant recorder and it's recording every sight, sound, smell, feeling, taste and sensation we have experienced since the very day we were born. Our subconscious mind also takes comments literally. That is why it is so important to monitor our self-talk and our sarcastic remarks. It is far better to say positive comments to others and to think nice thoughts about ourselves.

The subconscious mind also runs our bodily functions and our autonomic nervous system. We don't have to think about breathing, blinking, digesting our food or our heart pumping blood through our veins; these and more just happen unconsciously and automatically. When we give suggestions to and communicate with our subconscious mind, we can change our physiology, minimize pain, accelerate healing and slow down bleeding from a wound. I will share more about this in a later section.

Between the ages of seven and eleven, a barrier forms in our conscious mind, called the "critical faculty of the conscious mind." It functions like a gatekeeper and judgment factor, always interpreting information from the past.

Our critical faculty asks us questions such as, "Has this happened to me before?" and "How do I respond?"

Picture three-year old Timmy reaching for something on a hot stove. Mom sees this and screams; he gets frightened and maybe a little burned, and decided then and there that he won't be making that mistake again. Young children function primarily in their subconscious mind and are most often in a light hypnotic state. That is why they are so imaginative and suggestible, and why they take whatever you say to them literally.

The subconscious mind is like a super computer, continually running scripts and programs. In fact, it's the most powerful computer in existence, because we invented computers. Some of our programs and patterns are positive in nature while others are self-sabotaging. Normally when we purchase a computer, it comes with a very large operations manual. Consider this book as your mind's operations manual. Once you know more about how your mind works, you can create new patterns so that you are more in control of your emotions and behaviors. When you are feeling good and are in control, you can more effectively create the life that you want. And you can do this in all areas of your life. Another great benefit is you can also influence those around you in a positive way.

How information gets into the Subconscious

By now you are probably wondering how these scripts and programs get into our mind. Our programs, or our beliefs, get into our subconscious mind through a variety of ways. The subconscious mind is an associating mechanism, so any two things that happen close together or at the same time may get linked up automatically: fears, phobias and even some allergies.
According to immunologist Dr. Michael Levi, an allergy is like a *"phobia"* of the immune system.

Suggestions from Authority Figures

Another way programs become embedded in our mind is through comments or suggestions by authority figures, either knowingly or accidentally. If a teacher or doctor says something to us and we believe it to be true, then it can manifest in our mind. Let's say a school teacher gets annoyed with a student for not turning in her homework on time and then says to the student "you'll always be a procrastinator- you're never going to amount to much." As the child grows up they may continue to cycle through that negative thought of "I am never going to amount to much," and because of this they may end up sabotaging themselves. As adults, we may or may not be aware of the comments that were said to us as children, and those comments, whether negative or positive, are affecting our lives today.

Suggestions from Family and Friends

We also adopt behaviors from family members and friends. It's human nature to want to fit in and be accepted and loved and so many times people will adopt the same beliefs as their family, not even giving consideration to whether what they belief or don't believe is proven with evidence. Heredity is less predominant than previously thought, and many times ailments stem more from the environment than from heredity. More often than not people will have the same eating behaviors or exercise patterns as their parents or siblings. Often, our parents have rewarded us with food for good behavior or told us to eat everything on our plate. This can sometimes cause eating disorders and weight issues later in life.

Suggestions through Sensitizing Events

Behaviors are also established through sensitizing events in our life. If we are in a highly emotional state, for example, our subconscious mind is more open to suggestions, and if two things happen close together in time, as previously mentioned, they can automatically get linked up. This is how fears and phobias develop. Here is an example: a four-year-old walks into the kitchen where Mom is cooking, Mom sees a mouse, screams hysterically, and runs out of the room. From this experience the child may learn that mice are something to be afraid of.

We come into this world with only two innate fears, the fear of loud noises and the fear of falling. All other fears are learned behaviors. (Bandler 2008). This is why some people are scared of mice, others are scared of cockroaches, and some people are scared of birds. If these animals were to be feared, then everyone would be scared of the same ones.

Surprisingly, it is not so much the events that happen in life that is the cause of our problems; it is our *perception* of the event. A few years ago, a pilot for a commercial airline company had one of his engines die because it experienced a "bird strike." Birds got sucked into the engine as the plane was ascending causing the engine to die. The pilot, Captain C. B. "Sully" Sullenberger, successfully landed the large airplane with 155 passengers aboard onto the Hudson River in New York City. All the passengers and crew made it out to safety. One plane and one event. One hundred and fifty-five people and one hundred and fifty- five different responses. There were people who flew the next day and made the mental decision that the chances of their ever being in a plane accident again were probably slim and next-to- none. And some of the other passengers are probably still in therapy today. We can all agree that experiencing that event would be terribly frightening and traumatic; however, it is our choice of thoughts that will determine how we will move forward and experience our life. John Smith, CEO of XYZ Company, is obviously an educated and accomplished businessman; however, he is extremely uncomfortable speaking before an audience and he doesn't know why. When he was in the third grade, the teacher called him up in front of the class and asked him to write the word "cat" on the chalkboard. And so little Johnny wrote out the word "kat," and the teacher scolded him for spelling it incorrectly; all the children laughed as he walked back to his desk. Even though he may not consciously recall this particular incident, it has remained in his subconscious mind and because of this he feels anxiety and sweats excessively when he has to speak in front of an audience.

Repetition takes information down to the subconscious

Repetition also takes information down to the subconscious level. The conscious mind can do very few things at once, and so tasks that are repetitious move to our subconscious and the behavior goes on autopilot. Some of these behaviors are helpful, such as driving a car, swimming and riding a bike. Initially we had to think about operating the vehicle, but soon the driving behavior went on autopilot. We started riding a bike with training wheels but then it became as easy and natural as walking.

Bad habits generally start off with behaviors of perceived benefit and then turn into maladaptive behaviors. The habit of cigarette smoking, for example, often starts with a perceived benefit of feeling cool, being rebellious, fitting in, bonding with peers, or looking grown up, but then the repetitive hand-to-mouth action turns into a maladaptive behavior after a short time.

Businesses advertise their products repetitiously so that we associate words, phrases and even sounds with their products. You may remember, "M'm, M'm, Good! M'm, M'm, Good! That's what Campbell's soup is, M'm, M'm, Good!" And we associate manufacturer's names with products: Kleenex tissues, Philadelphia cream cheese, and Kraft macaroni and cheese.

Hypnosis takes information into the subconscious

Hypnosis also takes information down to the subconscious level. Research shows that if you want to achieve a goal, hypnosis can be more effective than therapy, because it deals directly with the *subconscious mind*, because that is where the negative program or problem exists.

The majority of time we run on autopilot and when we talk we influence situations whether we are trying to or not. My words may have influenced the following example without me realizing it.

Years ago on Halloween eve, I woke up around 1 a.m. because of shouting outside. I looked out my window and noticed in the parking lot across the street some late night partygoers were getting into a heated dispute that was escalating into a fistfight. Of course, I wanted it to end soon and peacefully so that no one would get hurt and then I could go back to sleep. So I opened my window and screamed, "Knock it off!" I had just been studying the power of words, so I was disappointed that my choice of words had a bit of a violent connotation. Immediately after I realized that "Cool it!" or "Hey, mellow out!" would have been more appropriate and effective choices.

Throughout the book I offer examples of better ways of communicating. The examples can go on and on, however you'll get the idea and the structure, so that you can easily and naturally begin speaking in a more positive and persuasive manner. Keep in mind that most of us were not brought up knowing how to speak positively or persuasively, so this takes some thought and practice. Remember also to be kind and patient with yourself; in a later section you will learn the importance of monitoring your self-talk.

Mark Twain said the difference between the right word and almost the right word is "the difference between lightning and a lightning bug." Twain had an incredible knack for nicely summing it all up, didn't he?

Section Two

How Our Words Can Influence a Medical Situation

With your new understanding of how the mind works and how powerful words can be, you may be wondering or wanting to learn more about how words can affect our physiology.

In the previous chapter I discussed how suggestions can be embedded in the subconscious mind through authority figures. Medical professionals, including doctors, nurses, and paramedics, are generally perceived as authority figures by the majority of the public. What they say to us in a crisis situation, or even during a regular routine doctor's visit, can affect us either positively or negatively. How we respond emotionally and physically also depends on how we interpret what they have said. Positively phrased sentences can help us heal more quickly, while poorly-stated words can hurt or hinder our recovery. Generally, children view parents as authority figures. Because of this, parents can many times influence how their child will behave in an emergency situation.

Many people are familiar with what is known as "The Placebo Effect," which is the power of positive suggestion. The word "placebo" is Latin for "I will please." Here is the example of a placebo most people are familiar with: During medical research, one test group of people will be given real medication and another group will be given a placebo pill, also referred to as a "sugar pill" and it has no medicinal value. Neither group is aware of which pill has been given to them. Research shows that the success rate of a placebo can be as high as 35 to 80 percent. This proves that because the person *believed* the medicine was real, the healing took place, and shows the power of the body to heal when armed with the positive belief that it will.

Not surprisingly, on the flip side of a placebo, is a "nocebo," which is a negative suggestion. The word nocebo is Latin for "I will be harmful." Generally when people say a nocebo, I don't think they do so knowingly or maliciously; they are just unaware of the power of negative language. Unfortunately, we all say and receive nocebos more often than we think.

(http://en.wikipedia.org/wiki/Placebo)

An example of a nocebo would be a doctor telling a patient that the shot they are about to receive is going to hurt or be painful. Saying the word pain actually gives the suggestion that pain is to be expected.

Placebos, or more commonly known as a positive suggestion, can work especially well with young children because children live more in the subconscious mind. Perhaps that is why children are so imaginative and impressionable. Parents interacting with their young children are actually using what is referred to as "waking hypnosis." You may have observed or done the following waking hypnotic suggestion yourself: A child gets a "boo-boo," and mommy or daddy offers to kiss it and make it all better. This is an example of a waking hypnotic suggestion; it works well in helping restore a sense of security and calmness in a young child.

In this section are a few simple examples of ways to phrase sentences so that you can offer verbal first aid in a crisis. If you are intrigued and want to learn more about verbal first aid, then I highly recommend reading *The Worst is Over* (Acosta &Prager 2002)

Here's the scenario:

Your toddler is running and slips and falls on some wet tile. You have determined it is not a serious fall, and the child looks at you and seems undecided as to how to react.

Say this: "You're okay; it's all right, you're fine."

Not that: "Stop your crying! I've told you not to run!"

Here is a variation on that scenario:

Your toddler is running and slips and falls down on some wet tile. If you see that your child is bleeding and in need of medical attention, you will serve the child better if you remain calm.

Say this: "I can see that you've hurt your arm. It's okay to cry. We are going to help you get better. Will you let mommy/daddy do that?"

Not that: "Oh, my God, I think you've broken your arm!"

In the previous situation you can also ask if other parts of their body are all right; focus on the parts that are obviously okay and positively acknowledge that it is good that their leg is okay, and so on. After getting the necessary medical attention, you can even say, "The worst is over and your body can begin to heal now."

The next two statements basically say the same thing, but one is said in a more positive way that may lead to a more positive outcome.

Here the scenario:

A doctor is sharing some information with a patient.

He/she should say this: "Although you have cancer, 60 percent of the people that have this type of cancer survive."

He/she should not say: "I am sorry to inform you that you have cancer and 40 percent of the people that have this type of cancer die from it."

As mentioned before, so much depends upon how we process and interpret what is being said to us. Some people will accept the doctor's negative statement and will say in their mind, "With my luck I'll be in that 40 percent." Others will think to themselves, "I am not going to die from cancer, I'll fight this! I am a survivor!" A better way to think, don't you agree?

The following scenarios demonstrate how you can help in a variety of emergency situations.

*Remember always call to 911 immediately, or firmly direct someone else to do it for you. Make sure you get acknowledgement from the person whom you have chosen to make the call.

Here's the scenario:

If you come upon a person who is unconscious, again first and foremost, make sure emergency help is on the way. If you are trained in CPR and first aid, then move forward with what you can physically do to help the person.

*Here what you can do verbally:

Say this: "Stay with me; stay with the sound of my voice."

Not that: "Oh, my God, please don't die! Don't die on me!"

Since the autonomic nervous system runs the body, we can change our own physiology, or the physiology of an ill or injured person, with a few well-chosen words. When we are in an accident or in a highly emotional state, our subconscious mind is more open to suggestions. The critical faculty of the conscious mind, which is the barrier or gatekeeper to the subconscious mind, is open and receptive to instructions as to what to do when we are in an accident or other traumatic situation.

An accident or a startle can open the critical faculty; so if we know the right words to say to someone who is injured, frightened, or distressed, we can help them change the experience to one that is less frightening or less traumatic. Because when we are communicating with the subconscious mind, we are communicating directly with the autonomic nervous system that directs the bodily functions. We can give suggestions for their breathing to slow down and for their body to relax. Once they are relaxed, their heart rate will slow down, as will any bleeding.

In an emergency situation where someone has taken control and is firmly giving directions as to what to do, the injured person experiences a sense of relief and, thus, will feel safer, become emotionally calmer, and even begin the healing process right there at the scene of the accident.

Here's the scenario

You arrive at the scene of a car accident; you decide to go over to the driver, who is sitting on the curb and is visibly shaken.

Say this: "The worst is over. The ambulance is on the way. My name is _____, and I can help you feel more comfortable. Would that be all right?"

Not that: "Wow! Did you see how smashed that car is? Oh, my God. But, don't worry; it's going to be okay, chill out."

If you make the negative statement above, you will more than likely agitate the person, because they will probably start thinking, "I am injured, confused, and hurt, and everything is NOT fine, so YOU chill out!"

Here's the scenario if the person is bleeding:

Say this: "The worst is over. The ambulance is on the way. My name is _____, and I can help you feel more comfortable. Will you do as I say?" And then say: "Once your blood has cleaned the wound you can stop your bleeding and save your blood." (Acosta &Prager 2002)

Not that: "Oh, my God, look at all that blood! It's going everywhere."

If the person is bleeding but unconscious, you can also say that help is on the way and follow with the positive statement above. The subconscious mind hears everything, so even though the person may appear to be unconscious and not coherent, their subconscious mind is hearing your words. Sometimes in an altered state, the mind is even more acutely aware of what is going on around us. So even if you think that the unconscious person cannot hear you, stay away from questionable comments, such as, "Do you think they will make it?"

Research has shown that patients who have been anesthetized and undergone surgery can sometimes consciously recall music that was being played in the background or certain things that were said by the physicians (Goleman 1989). Amazingly, in hypnosis a post-surgery patient can recall verbatim what was said while under anesthesia. As mentioned before, the unconscious/subconscious mind is a recorder and it remembers every sight, sound, smell, feeling, taste, and sensation from the day we were born.

Here's the scenario:

We are administering first aid or medical treatment and we want to find out how much pain or discomfort the person we are tending to is in:

Say this: "On a scale from one to ten, ten being extremely uncomfortable and one being completely comfortable, what is your comfort level?"

Not that: "How bad is the pain? Is it unbearable? Is it the worst pain you've had in your life?"

Avoid the word "pain," as it gives the suggestion and expectation that there will be pain.

Here's the scenario:

I recently went for a diagnostic mammogram. The well-meaning lab technician said, "I know that's an excruciatingly tight pinch," and she would apologize, because she was well-meaning and didn't want me to suffer. I did my best to ignore her comments. Here is what she could have said to make the experience more comfortable.

Say this: "I know a way to make this as comfortable for you as possible. Would you like for me to share with you how to do this?" (If the person agrees then you can move forward with the following)

Say this: "Close your eyes and take a deep breath and as you exhale imagine yourself in a place that you would rather be- some place that brings about a relaxing feeling -and just imagine yourself there." (Disassociation will provide more comfort.) From here you can have the person continue to use their imagination with suggestions of relaxation and comfort at the peaceful place they've chosen.

The subconscious mind cannot tell the difference between reality and the imagination. If someone imagines something vividly in their mind, their body will respond as if that something is actually happening. For example, if you imagine that your hand is in a bucket of icy cold water and you imagine that it is starting to tingle and become numb, you will create this experience in your hand. This technique is useful for someone who has been in an accident and has been burned.

There is an abundance of research that's proven that if you give suggestions for coolness to a person who has been burned within the first four hours of the burn, the person will heal more quickly and there will be less chance of infection and scarring, because the cooling suggestions will reduce the inflammation response that causes the scarring.

Before ether, or chemical anesthesia, was developed, the mortality rate for major surgery was high. It has been reported that the mortality

(http://www.time.com/time/magazine/article/0, 9171,823748,00.html)

rate of major surgery was about 50 percent. In the early 1800s, Dr. James Esdaile probably performed more surgical operations under hypnoanesthesia than any other physician even to this day. He took out grapefruit size tumors, performed amputations, and did many other surgical procedures using hypnosis. Those who opposed him said that his patients who had undergone operations were just pretending not to hurt. "In 161 cases operated on by Esdaile (using hypnotic techniques), mortality dropped to five percent, and in none of the fatal cases was death an immediate outcome of surgery."

Pain is the body's signal that something needs to be attended to, so seek the necessary medical attention right away. Suggestions for comfort and quick healing can be given as an adjunct to a physician's care.

Finally, if there is an emergency situation and you are in doubt as to what to say, then it may be best to say nothing at all; just be there for the injured person and offer comfort by holding their hand, if appropriate.

(http://en.wikipedia.org/wiki/James_Esdaile)

Section Three

For Teachers and Sales Professionals

Personally and professionally it's been proven that a few well-chosen words can create a positive impression and help people feel good about you. And the right words can also help people feel better about who they are, as well as influence them to take action or make a buying decision.

When working with people there are ways to offer guidance, or "creative criticism," without hurting a person's pride or self-esteem. Human beings are creatures of emotion and keeping this in mind there are still ways to say what needs to be said, without stepping on any toes.

If you want to support, encourage and inspire those around you then choosing to focus on a person's strengths versus their weaknesses is very important in creating a good impression and developing a relationship. When you are speaking to a loved one or potential customer, keep a person's feelings first and foremost. Research shows that people who have high self-esteem are generally happier, healthier, and more productive in life both personally and professionally.

A word of advice in regards to giving advice: It is important not to use the word "BUT." That's right, the *but* word. When you say "but," it negates the first half of your sentence.

I love this example: "Your wife is lovely, "but . . ." As you can see, you have no place to go from here!

Here's the Scenario:

You are a sales manager and you need your salesperson to be more proactive in contacting potential and existing clients:

Say this: "You're doing a great job and your clients love to hear from you, so please make the time to call them a little more often; this will help you boost your bottom-line, as well!"

Not that: "You're doing a great job around here, BUT you don't follow up enough with your clients."

Here's the Scenario:

You are a voice coach and one of your students is occasionally singing off-key.

Say this: "You have a great voice and with continued practice your voice will develop even more beautifully."

Not that: "You have a great voice BUT you sometimes hit the wrong notes."

Here's the scenario:

As a teacher or a coach you may have to ask people questions about why they behave in a certain manner. Of course, you want them to be truthful with both you and themselves so that you can help them. So if you feel that they are not being forthcoming you may want to:

Say this: "You need to be honest with yourself."

Not that: "When are you going to stop lying to yourself?"

Here's the scenario:

You are an athletic coach and one of your football players keeps throwing the football a little too far to the left.

Say this: "Wow! You've got a powerful throw, and if you turn your hips a little this way, you'll find that the ball will go right where you want it to go."

Not that: "If you can't throw that ball straight by the end of this practice, you're going to be on the bench this season."

Here's the scenario:

You are an athletic coach and you are training an athlete for an upcoming competition.

Say this: "As you throw the ball, imagine it going into the hoop over and over again. Imagine holding the first place trophy over your head!"

Not that: "No pain, no gain. If you don't press yourself harder, you won't have a chance at that trophy."

Here's the scenario:

You are an athletic coach and you are pushing your athletes to train even harder.

Say this: "You can do it! Go for it! You can do it! Keep it up! Imagine that you've already reached your goal!"

Not that: "Don't quit! Are you a quitter? No player of mine quits!"

We understand what the word "don't" means. However, when we say the word *don't*, our attention and focus shift to the thing we are <u>not</u> supposed to do. The subconscious mind does not process the word "don't," so in the above scenario with the coach, the athlete is hearing, "Quit, quit, quit!"

As adults we understand when someone says, "Don't touch the stove; it's hot," because we learned this as a child. You probably realize that your attention has now shifted to the fact that the stove is hot.

We get what we focus on. You can test this theory right now. Don't think of the color red; don't notice the red stop signs or the red cars or red roses. What are thinking about now? RED. Another example would be someone who wants to stop smoking and they keep repeating to themselves, "I don't want to smoke." But the mind is hearing, "I want to smoke." The auto-suggestion that the person should be reinforcing is what they actually want, which is to be a non-smoker or smoke-free: "I am now a non-smoker; I am smoke-free."

Here's the scenario:

You are a teacher and one of your students is getting A's on their homework and papers, but they are not well-spoken when they get up in front of the class.

Say this: "You are an excellent student; your work is outstanding, and with a little coaching your presentation skills will be exceptional as well."

Not that: "Well, you won't be making your living as a public speaker."

Remember, when we are speaking—whether we are a parent, a teacher or a sales- person—there is someone listening to our words, and they are translating what we say in their mind and thinking, "How do I respond?" or "What does this mean to me?" or "What is in it for me?" Sales professionals call this *Station WIIIFM*.

It is important to keep WIIIFM in mind when speaking with people. Human beings are emotional creatures, so we are strongly influenced by how we feel. Because of this, you want to appeal to the emotions. Our subconscious mind is the seat of our imagination and emotions, so to be more influential, you will want to appeal to a person's senses by incorporating their imagination and feelings.

People are listening to what you say and interpreting it, and they may think you have said something different or meant something different than what you actually said or meant. And this happens even though both of you are speaking the same language!

When shoppers make purchases, their buying decisions are based on how they think the particular product is going to make them feel. We may associate feelings of success and power with the purchase of a Mercedes, a Lexus, or a Rolex watch. Or we may consider ourselves ecologically friendly if we drive a more efficient car versus a gas-guzzler. We make decisions based on emotions, not necessarily on what we need and generally not on logic.

You have probably heard of activating a potential customer's "hot buttons"? You know, touching on those emotions that will get them to buy your product or service. How do you find out what these hot buttons, or emotional triggers, are? You simply ask them. And here's how:

Here's the scenario:

You are a car salesperson and a prospect walks onto the lot. First, smile and make a statement that is agreeable and true. If it is a lovely day, then say, "It's a lovely day, isn't it?"

After some rapport has been established if they haven't yet let on as to what excites them, then:

Say this: "What is important to you in a car or vehicle"? (You can replace the underlined words with the product or service you represent: "What's important to you in a computer?")

Not that: "Can I sell you a car?" or "Are you interested in buying a car today?"

What the prospects share with you are their hot buttons. You may hear such things as safety, performance, value, and more. Once you have this valuable information, you will be able to appeal to their desires.

Here's the scenario:

You are a business or sales professional and you have done a presentation for a potential client who needs your product or services. If you feel that your client is ready to make a buying decision, you can attempt to close the sale by employing a "double bind," also known as the "illusion of choice," because either option creates the same result for the person doing the speaking.

Say this: "Would you like to get started on Monday or Tuesday?"

Not that: "Well, you'll probably just want to think about it and then give me a call."

You could also say this: "Would you like to use Visa or MasterCard?"

Not that: "Do you want to buy this?"

For another choice you could say this: "The sooner you <u>take care of the paperwork</u>, the sooner you <u>can drive home with your new car!</u>" (You can change the underlined parts as the situation applies.)

As you can see in the examples, the sooner a person completes the task, the sooner they can enjoy the benefit. So you can fill in the blanks according to your circumstances: "**The sooner you _____, the sooner you can _____.**"

<u>Here's the scenario</u>:

You are a salesperson making phone calls to set appointments.

Say this: "Ms. Business Owner, I have helped other business owners like yourself grow their businesses by 20%. Perhaps we can help you achieve similar results. Can we meet either Tuesday or Wednesday of next week? Which do you prefer?

Not that: "Next month we are doing an advertising section in our newspaper on your particular type of business; do you want to buy an ad?"

Here's the scenario:

You are a salesperson in a meeting presenting your products to a potential customer.

Say this: "I would like to <u>share</u> with you how, by working together, we can help you increase your business by 20%." Or "I would like to <u>show</u> you how you can benefit." Or: "I would like to share with you how you can benefit."

Not that: "Let me tell you about our distribution; it is much better than our competitors'."

Here's the scenario:

Your customer is on the edge of making a buying decision. When encouraging others to make a decision that is in their best interest, have them step into the picture of themselves experiencing the benefit.

Say this: "Imagine how good you will feel driving around town in your new car; so let's take care of the details so that you can do just that."

Not that: "Once you sign the contract, you can drive this baby off the lot."

When a salesperson is presenting products or services to potential customers, the customer can sense if the salesperson has a hidden agenda and is more interested in making a sale than in helping them make a choice that is in their best interest.

Sales professionals with a high level of integrity and the customer's best interest in the forefront will do exceptionally well, because they will receive an abundance of referrals.

When presenting features of our products it comes across as more credible if we say it in the following way.

Say this: Studies show that this particular computer system is excellent for people who are relatively new to using computers."

Not that: "If you are computer illiterate, this is the one for you."

And if you want to make the above statement even more persuasive, you can give a reason why. Research shows that people are more agreeable and willing to follow through on taking action if they are given a reason why, even if it does not make logical sense. Just use the word "because"!

Say this: "Studies have shown that this particular computer system is excellent for people who are just learning to use a computer for the first time, **because** the software system was developed with first-time users in mind."

Not that: "Here is the computer that most beginners buy."

(http://www.artofblog.com/because- a-power- word/)

While the previous *Not that* statement is neither terribly offensive nor unpleasant, you can see that the **Say this** statement is more professional and persuasive.

For variety, you can switch out the following words as needed: "Experience shows," "Research shows," and "Studies show." The reason these statements are effective is because they are not your opinion but the opinion of others who are experts in the field!

It is human nature to love to know the reasons behind why we should have something or do something. So share with the person you are speaking with what the reasons are.

Here's the scenario:

You are a car salesperson, and the car you are showing a has a higher ticket price than another car; however, it gets much better mileage than the less expensive car that your customer is also looking over.

Say this: "This car gets 40 miles to the gallon, <u>which means you will save money at the gas pump.</u>

Not that: "This car gets great gas mileage, but it is more expensive."

Or in the scenario with the computer you could:

Say this: "You might already be aware of the fact that <u>Mac computers generally remain virus free</u>."

Not that: "This computer is less likely to get a virus, but it is more expensive."

n the previous examples, you can fill in the nderlined portions, depending on your roduct or service. People become alert when ou say that they might be aware of something. nd if they weren't aware of it before, they are ow!

Section Four

Parents and Partners

Have you ever noticed that some people speak more courteously to strangers than they do to family members? Because of society's expectations, many people, not all, will use good manners with restaurant servers, yet at home they will speak harshly to their children or spouses, telling them what to do instead of politely asking for what they want. The best way to teach others how to treat us, is to treat them with respect and courtesy.

Most of us were not brought up knowing better ways to phrase our sentences.

Who hasn't heard the cliché, "Sticks and stones may break my bones but words will never hurt me"? Verbal abuse can cause much more damage than physical abuse, because people carry emotional baggage with them for years, and sometimes even a lifetime. So, if we hurt a person's feelings, the best thing to do is to offer a sincere apology. And we need to be kind to ourselves as well, whenever we make mistakes.

To keep peace and love in our relationships with family, friends, and even strangers, it is best to focus on the positive. Look for, see, and acknowledge the best in others, and focus on what you appreciate about them and what you value in the relationship.

Whatever we send our energy to and focus on continues to grow. So metaphorically speaking water the flowers in your garden.

Here's the scenario:

Your husband keeps forgetting to take out the trash and is neglectful in helping around the house.

Say this: "Honey, I am thankful that you help around the house. May I kindly ask you to please take out the trash?"

Not that: "It really makes me mad that you don't care about me or about helping around the house."

Here's the scenario:

Your wife is spending too much time at the office and you want some quality time with her.

Say this: "Honey, I really enjoy spending time with you, so can we schedule some time together?"

Not that: "You care more about your work than you care about me and the family."

Here's the scenario:

Your spouse sometimes runs late and doesn't call to let you know that they are running late.

Say this: "I care about you and I appreciate when you call to let me know that you are going to be late."

Not that: "It really gets me angry when you are late. You are so inconsiderate, all you care about is yourself."

Remember the saying, "You can attract more flies with honey than you can with vinegar." And so show your loved ones and people in general, that they are appreciated. Make them feel good about themselves and they will be more open to your positive suggestions and guidance. What we appreciate "appreciates" and the more love we give the more love we will receive in all areas of our life.

Here's the scenario:

In daily life you want to be more influential with your children.

Say this: "Honey (of course, the endearment is optional), **the sooner you** finish your homework, **the sooner you** can go outside and play."

(You can change the underlined portion to fit the situation.)

Not that: "Finish your homework or you'll be grounded for a week!"

Or you can,

Say This: "**The sooner you** clean your room, the sooner you can play with your toys.

Not that: "Clean your room or you'll lose your phone and TV privileges for a week!"

Here's the scenario:

Your child is running and horsing around the swimming pool.

Say this: "please walk around the pool. I can see you're having fun. Do you want to continue to play at the swimming pool?" Get agreement from them.

After they say, "Yes" you can say, "if you want to continue having fun then you are going to have to walk around the pool, would you please do that? The first yes should get you the second yes and cooperation.

Not that: "Don't run, if you run we are going to have to leave."

Here's the scenario:

Your five-year-old is heading for your new couch with a full glass of grape juice.

Say this: "Mommy wants you to come over and sit **right here** and get all of that delicious grape juice into your mouth."

Not that: "Don't you dare sit down on my new couch with that grape juice!"

Here's the scenario:

Your child brings home a B on his report card.

Say this: "I am proud of you. You are so intelligent and capable of B's and even A's. Is there anyway we can help to support you even more in your learning?"

Not that: "No child of mine gets B's you can do better than that. Bring home all A's next time."

Or, another way to handle this situation is to simply acknowledge their intelligence and their wonderful "B"! The reality is that a grade of "B" is above average. There is no need to make your child feel that while they did good, they

didn't do good enough. A child who really wants to learn and finds their grades to be important will often open the door by being disappointed and saying something like, "But I really wanted an "A". That is a verbal cue for you to take the conversation further. If they don't say something like this then smile, congratulate them, and celebrate their wonderful "B".

Here's the scenario:

Your child keeps forgetting to brush her teeth.

Say this: "Remember to brush your teeth, that way you keep eating the foods you like.

Not that: "If I told you once, I've told you a million times!! Go brush your teeth. If you don't brush your teeth, there will be no more candy for you."

And remember to never reinforce good behaviors with food. Many parent use candy and treats as a reward for good behavior. This may lead to eating disorders in the future. Food is to give us energy and nutrition. If you want to reinforce a positive behavior then learn what excites and motivates your child. Praise, love and approval many times are the ultimate reward.

Here's the scenario:

Your five-year-old is playing too rough with your one-year-old. This can be adjusted to fit the situation. Perhaps you've just got a new puppy and your child is pulling the dog's tail and playing too rough. And if you need to take action quickly it is okay to insert "Stop Now." Say the child's name and then "Stop Now" and then follow with the saying below.

Say this: "child's name, Stop Now...we need to be gentle with your little sister, okay?" (Get agreement by nodding your head and you can even demonstrate what a gentle touch is like.)

Not that: "Hey, knock it off, stop it, stop being so rough with the baby."

It is emotionally harmful to your children if you compare them to one another. People have their own special talents, skills and gifts. We need to focus on what is positive in a person versus the negative. Comparing children to their siblings causes emotional problems and resentment.

Here's the scenario:

Your daughter is excelling in sports and your son is doing well academically.

Say this: "We are thankful to have two such intelligent and talented children."

Not that: "Well, one of you has the coordination, and the other one has the smarts."

Even if the above example is said in a light-hearted and joking manner, such comments can have negative effects. As seemingly trivial as the above examples may seem, because of stress and upbringing, intelligent people are saying comments like these to their loved ones every day.

Here's the scenario:

Your child takes a plate of food and is heading into the living room to sit in front of the television.

Say this: Please sit here at the table and do you prefer to sit in the chair that faces the TV or the one that faces the window?

Not that: "You know you are not allowed to sit in front of the TV while eating!"

You can use the illusion of choice by offering two choices that are acceptable to you just by saying, "Do you prefer _____ or _____?" This gives the person the feeling that they are the one making the decision.

All adults and children want to feel that they have some level of control over their lives. The illusion of choice can create this feeling, so offer choices that are still in alignment with what you want to accomplish.

Section Five

Things We Silently Say to Ourselves

From the beginning of this book you have probably been wondering what was said to me to turn my weight problem around. When I was 21, a new friend and very attractive man, whom I respected, said to me, "You are what you think you are." Well, I was a bit self-conscious because I was about 15 pounds overweight by my own standards, even though he thought I looked sexy and beautiful. He told me to look into the mirror every day and say to myself, "You are beautiful." In his eyes I was beautiful. And so I did what he instructed me to do and I started affirming it on a daily basis. Within a short period of time I began feeling more beautiful and confident. And people were commenting on how beautiful I looked, so I thought, "Wow, this right-thinking stuff really works!" Actually, when our self-esteem and confidence levels are high, we become more attractive because our inner beauty shines through.

When I was in my early twenties, a friend of mine in real estate sales introduced me to a very famous book, *Think and Grow Rich,* by Napoleon Hill. If you haven't yet read this Depression Era classic from the 1930s, I highly recommend it. Hill had been encouraged by billionaire Andrew Carnegie to interview the richest men in the United States and find out their principles of success, because even though there were many people struggling, there were also people prospering. The book is condensed into thirteen principles, one of them being *autosuggestion,* the conversation we have going on in our head. Also referred to as "self-talk," it is the silent conversation we continually have with ourselves.

With our self-talk, many of us unknowingly create our own reality by reinforcing positive or negative behaviors and beliefs, ultimately giving ourselves the results that we get in life. If we focus on or think of something that might happen and then it actually happens, we refer to it as a "self- fulfilling prophecy," whether the event is good or bad. It's important to realize that we are hypnotizing ourselves with our own autosuggestions.

As mentioned before, we can be strongly influenced by authority figures. And we are an authority when it comes to our thoughts about ourselves, are we not? We most certainly are.

Most of us live fairly patterned or repetitious lives, and although it is not exactly the same thing day in and day out, we do have our routine thoughts and rituals that contribute to our conditioned behaviors, as well. If we are thinking something, and we believe it to be true, then it can manifest or develop in our life. You have probably heard the saying, "You are what you think you are." Actually, you can be so much more if you start using your mind more effectively, by focusing your thoughts on what you want and then taking action to make those things happen.

Often we are recycling the same old negative self-talk. We are naturally supposed to be feeling joyful, successful, and happy. If we are not, it's because we are running negative programs in our subconscious minds.

Sometimes we know consciously the negative things we are saying to ourselves, but at other times we are not aware of the negative thoughts just churning beneath the surface. These thoughts can hold us back from achieving the goals we set, and slow us down or even prevent us from creating the life we desire.

Here is a list of some of the negative thoughts people say to themselves and others:

- Everyone is struggling in this economy.
- Life is hard or life is a struggle.
- Nobody has any money.
- I can't remember names.
- My memory is terrible.
- I can't sleep; insomnia runs in my family.
- You're not a rocket scientist.
- I hate my thighs/body.
- You drive me crazy/I am going crazy.
- I attract losers.
- I have a slow metabolism.
- I am not the sharpest tack in the drawer.
- You're not as good as you think you are.
- Money is the root of all evil.
- Rich people are greedy.
- Money doesn't grow on trees.
- I just look at food and get fat.
- Over the lips and to the hips.
- I am not smart enough.
- I am not good enough.
- I don't deserve him/her.
- Bad things always happen to me.
- You're giving me a heart attack.

And the notorious "I am worried sick!" it's no wonder that 40% to 80% of the people in hospitals are there because of stress-related illnesses.

Do you know someone who tells you that there are no jobs out there, that nobody is making any money, that you can't make money in the stock market, and so on? If you have to be around someone that talks like this, then do some filtering with what you will accept and allow into your mind. Remember, *like attracts like*, so protect your precious good thoughts! And learn to reframe the negative thoughts with more positive thoughts: The glass is half *full* rather than half empty—it's a matter of perception.

From a previous section you may remember that our subconscious minds do not process "don't," so be aware of negative self-talk or autosuggestions.

Here's the scenario:

You are sitting in your car in traffic and it's hot and uncomfortable and you are worrying that you are going to be late for an appointment.

Say this: "I am feeling calmer and more relaxed with each breathe that I take."

Not that: "I *don't* want to have stress." or "I *don't* want to feel anxious or out of control."

Have you ever found yourself saying that you are going to try harder or are going to try to do better? Or do you know someone who says they are going to "try" and do something rather than they are "going to" do something? The word *try* actually implies failure. Think about it: We either do something or we don't.

Here's the Scenario:

The next time you want to commit to doing something such as showing up to an important appointment on time,

Say this: "I am *going to* do it." You will feel better when you say it this way and you will experience more success.

Not that: "I am going to *try* and do it."

Many people think and feel that they are not good enough, not smart enough, or not worthy of abundance, success, or love. Negative self-talk may include: "I am a failure, a loser, lazy, weak," etc. You get the idea.

What should we be affirming? We should be repetitiously affirming the opposite of the negative self-talk. Autosuggestions should include: I am more than good enough, I am worthy, I am lovable, I am capable, I am intelligent, and so on. Whatever the negative statement is, we need to flip it around into a positive.

An associate of mine had a strong desire to become a motivational speaker. Now he was actually a very good public speaker, yet he could not motivate himself to get off the couch and do the things he needed to do to create the life he wanted. After some question-and-answer time together, we uncovered that, even though he looked the part of a successful businessman and had the skill and talent to give talks, at his subconscious level he was hearing the words, "I am a failure." Through our discussion he came to the realization that this negative self-talk had become embedded in his subconscious mind by his ex-wife's constant screaming at him: "You're a failure as a father and you're a failure as a husband."

The subconscious mind is a magnificent doer. It is like a magic genie and it takes our comments literally, which can be unfortunate for those of us who have a sarcastic sense of humor!

Here are some comments that we often make jokingly but that, unfortunately, our subconscious takes literally: "I just look at food and I get fat," or "a moment on the lips but forever on the hips." So many people have shared with me that when they were at their most slender, they actually thought they were fat. Then once the weight came on, they would look back at pictures of themselves when they were slender and healthy and finally realize that during that time in their lives they were actually thin, but they kept saying to themselves that they were fat. This is an example of our getting what we think about—a self-fulfilling prophecy. Who hasn't heard the saying, "Be careful what you wish for"? Obviously these people were not consciously wishing themselves fat; they just didn't clearly see and truly appreciate being the way they were, and they didn't know how powerful their minds could be when they affirmed something. This means that we need to be giving ourselves autosuggestions that we love being at our ideal weight of X number of pounds.

Here's the scenario:

We keep sabotaging our finances by saying and thinking the wrong things about money.

Say this: "Money is flowing freely and abundantly into my life now."

Not that: "I just want enough money to get by and pay my bills"

Here's the scenario:

We may be thinking or saying the following things to ourselves. And because the subconscious mind follows our directives, we may sabotage our body with self-talk. We want to stay away from such negative self-talk as: "He's giving me a heart attack," or "You cause my blood pressure to rise!"

Say this: "I am becoming healthier and more fit each day."

Not that: "I am so fat; I hate my thighs and my body."

Here's the scenario:

We sabotage our overall success with negative thoughts and autosuggestions about ourselves professionally and personally.

Say this: "I can accomplish anything I set my mind to."

Not that: "Because I don't have a good education, I'll never amount to much."

Many people traveling by airplane will complain about having to breathe the same canned air in the plane as the many other passengers; and they may even say that they always get sick when they travel. They then experience a self-fulfilling prophecy by getting sick for a few days after they have returned home. This is an example of giving ourselves a *nocebo*. Recently, I came across some very interesting research that showed that the air quality on a plane is actually much better than the air quality in most office buildings. On the airplane the air is continually being filtered and refreshed with the outside air during the flight. We can now affirm that we'll stay healthy when we travel.

I know of two situations where a person said they needed some time off from work, but instead of asking for time off they kept saying, "I need a break, I need a break." Within a short period of time each of them had a fall that resulted in a broken ankle. Have you ever heard someone say, "With my luck, it will happen to me"? Usually they are not talking about something positive like winning the lottery!

(http://www.msnbc.msn.com/id/41581445/ns/t ravel-seasonal_travel/)

We become what we think about and focus on, so if you are not currently living the life of your dreams, then I suggest that you do some self-reflection and figure out what it is you want in your life—how you want to think, feel, and behave in all areas of your life—your health, finances, and relationships. And then go for it, beginning right now.

Take the time to write out what you want to create in your life. Write it out as if you have already accomplished it, and allow yourself to experience the good feelings you'd have with those accomplishments. I recommend reading your creation list to yourself several times a day, because *what you think about, you bring about.*

And remember **the sooner you** get started, **the sooner you** will be on your way to a healthier, happier, and more prosperous life!

Bibliography

Daniel Goleman *Emotional Intelligence: Why It Can Matter More Than IQ* – 1996 page 3

1997 by Robert Dilts
http://www.nlpu.com/Articles/article9.htm
quotes Dr. Michael Levi Page 12

(Richard Bandler's Guide to Tranceformation. 2008) page 15

(http://en.wikipedia.org/wiki/Placebo) page 21

The Worst Is **Over**: What to Say When Every Moment Counts Judith Acosta, L.C.S.W. and Judith Simon **Prager**, Ph.D. 2002, page 29

Daniel Goleman 1989
http://www.nytimes.com/1989/10/26/us/health-psychology-doctors-find-that-surgical-patients-may-still-hear-despite.html
page 30

http://www.time.com/time/magazine/article/0,9171,823748,00.html Hypnosis for burns 1955, page 32

(http://en.wikipedia.org/wiki/James_Esdaile), page 33

(http://www.artofblog.com/because-a-power-word/) page 48

Think and Grow Rich by Napoleon Hill, page 64

(http://www.msnbc.msn.com/id/41581445/ns/travel-seasonal_travel/) page 74

About the Author

Mindy Ash is a Clinical Hypnotherapist and an Emotional Intelligence Coach. She is the owner of Hawaii Hypnosis Center in Honolulu.

Since 2006 she has helped hundreds of people to stop smoking, and has facilitated thousands of hypnosis sessions that have helped people to make positive changes in their lives.

Additionally she has lectured on hypnosis and conducted sales training classes for various private companies, hospitals and universities in Hawaii, Georgia and Southern California.

Mindy's television appearances include the Andy Bumatai Show, live on Oceanic Channel 16 and segments on Hawaii News Now as well as National syndicated American Now.

Speaking Engagements include:
- Kaiser Permanente
- Sharps Hospital Grossmont
- Hawaii Pacific University
- Kapiolani Community College
- Axa Financial Services
- Metropolitan Rotary of Honolulu
- FAMES

Additional Information

Ms. Ash offers phone consultations and coaching in person or over the phone. She speaks and educates at corporate events.

If you feel this book can help some people you know then let them know it's available at amazon.com.

Visit: www.hypnosisaudiostore.com or www.hawaiihypnosiscenter.com

Please send inquiries to:

Mindy Ash
350 Ward Ave., 106-283
Honolulu, HI 96814

808-221-7353

Made in the USA
San Bernardino, CA
02 November 2014